THE
LITTLE BOOK
OF
BUILDING
FIRES

THE
LITTLE BOOK
OF
BUILDING
FIRES

HOW TO CHOP, SCRUNCH, STACK & LIGHT A FIRE

SALLY COULTHARD

An Apollo Book

First published in the UK in 2017 by Head of Zeus Ltd
This paperback edition first published in 2022 by Head of Zeus Ltd,
part of Bloomsbury Publishing Plc

975312468

A CIP catalogue record for this book
is available from the British Library.

ISBN (PB) 9781803289908
ISBN (E) 9781786696489

Text design and typesetting by Ben Cracknell Studios

Printed and bound in Great Britain by
CPI Group (UK) Ltd, Croydon CR0 4YY

Head of Zeus Ltd
5–8 Hardwick Street
London EC1R 4RG

WWW.HEADOFZEUS.COM

For my brother Ben

Contents

Introduction

'Give me', said Joe, 'a good book, or a good newspaper, and sit me down afore a good fire and I ask no better.'

CHARLES DICKENS, *Great Expectations*

My oldest memories are touched by fire. The sweet smell of woodsmoke takes me straight back to my childhood home, a tall Victorian townhouse blessed with open fires on every floor.

I'd help Dad make and light the fire in the front room, a treat, because it was a space reserved for special occasions, and a great excuse to have him to myself. I learned by osmosis, slowly watching and absorbing the careful ritual of scrunching newspaper and arranging bone-dry twigs on a bed of ash. I especially liked it when he would hold a large sheet of newspaper over the mouth of the chimney to draw air up the flue. This adroit trick would transform a few infant flames into a roaring inferno in seconds – a feat both thrilling and the right side of deliciously dangerous.

Fire also takes me back to messing about outdoors as a child. My brother and I would sneak to the bottom of the garden, having smuggled out a box of matches, and while away dry afternoons building small campfires and setting fire to anything that came to hand. Our favourite game involved lighting long lengths of dried nettles, the stems of which would smoulder like a cigarette; we'd sit around the campfire, holding them aloft like socialite dandies, taking the occasional puff, quickly followed by a cough and splutter.

I equate fire with childhood holidays too. Family expeditions weren't always stress-free, but the best moments were the ones when we found ourselves around a campfire, or cooking outdoors. From rough French campsites to back-garden sleepovers with friends, evenings were always sweeter with an open fire and convivial conversation. We'd spend summers with an Italian family, making campfires in Alpine forests and cooking polenta in a huge copper pan over the embers – the careful preparation that went into making and tending the fire adding to the sense of occasion.

As an adult, my relationship with fire has mutated into something different, but no less intense. Fire has come to mean other things – romantic evenings huddled under a blanket, or the irresistible draw of a pub after a wet Sunday walk. As a young adult working in London, it was

heaven to escape for a few days to a remote bolthole, complete with open fire. Away from the city, I could pretend I was living a different life, the ritual of setting and lighting a fire making me feel calmer and more connected with nature. I'm never surprised when people put 'open fires' on their holiday cottage wish lists – a rural retreat without one seems strangely pointless.

Nowadays, I live on a farm with my young family. Fire, again, is everywhere. Bonfires are a regular event, a useful tool for clearing away the cuttings and branches that inevitably pile up. The kids have campfires in their little stretch of woodland – many a saucepan has been ruined by their attempts at hot chocolate, or failing that, they crack open a packet of marshmallows and perfect their toasting technique, which is something akin to a rotisserie.

Indoors, the farmhouse is warmed by a wood-fired biomass boiler – a temperamental affair but one that, when it works, puffs out gentle wafts of scented smoke, and leaves me feeling slightly less guilty about having the heating on. When the cold weather really sets in, however, no evening is complete without lighting up one of the wood burners or open fires. Wood-burning stoves are a completely different beast from traditional hearth fires, and it's taken a while to master the differences. What you miss in the friendly pops and crackles of an open flame, you more than get back in heat output and efficiency. I've discovered there's a place for both, and each has its charm.

There is, of course, a dark side to fire. As the old saying goes, 'Fire makes a good servant but a bad master', and the potential for things to go wrong is never far away. As a parent, I wince at the thought of my children 'playing' with fire the way my brother and I did, but those early lessons taught me more about the anatomy and behaviour of fire than any schoolroom.

And that's what this book is really about. Open fires and wood burners have made a glittering comeback in the past few years; there are lots of reasons why, both economic and environmental, but perhaps it's also true that central heating is, well, just a bit *soulless*, and not everything worth having can come at the push of a button.

In the same way that thousands of people are rediscovering the pleasure of local produce or the satisfaction of smallholding, so too are many of us rekindling the primeval pleasure of wood fires. The very act of collecting branches and chopping logs, scrunching up newspaper, building stacks and watching them burn, triggers deeply buried memories. It all feels just so *familiar*.

But for all this enthusiasm, how many of us know how to build a fire? Would we know which kinds of trees burn best or how long logs need to be stored? Could we make our own firelighters, or build the perfect fire stack? Most of us love to toast our toes by an open fire but don't know or have forgotten how to build one and keep it alight.

That's where *The Little Book of Building Fires* comes in. It's time to get back to some firecraft basics. By the end of this book, I hope you'll have a better grasp of sourcing, seasoning and storing firewood, choosing kindling and tinder, and building and lighting the perfect fire. There's also plenty about keeping safe – a lesson I've sometimes had to learn the hard way.

Nothing beats the companionable crackle of an open fire. In this world of fast-paced technology and virtual experiences, if we can stop and steal time for just one bit of slow living, let it be the enjoyment of a traditional wood fire. Build it, and you'll find yourself strangely drawn to the flames. You'll also feel compelled to sit, stay and talk for a while or warm your toes in comfortable silence. Above all, you'll be partaking in a ritual that's as old as humanity itself.

CHAPTER ONE

The Joy of Fire

'Love is a smoke raised
with the fume of sighs;
Being purged, a fire
sparkling in lovers' eyes'

WILLIAM SHAKESPEARE, *Romeo and Juliet*

The story of fire is at the very heart of who we are. Scratch the surface of the history of human endeavour, and there's a good chance you'll find a bed of embers at the bottom.

Humans are the only animals to have learned how to make fire at will. Our relationship with flames has been a long one; archaeology puts the earliest evidence of campfires a million years back, but we've been playing with fire for much longer than that. Recent studies have revealed that our primitive ape-like ancestors were probably opportunistic, scavenging 'firechasers', hanging around the edges of forest fires to grab fleeing prey or pick among their cooked remains. They would have also seen the new plant growth springing up after the smoke cleared and understood the power of fire to both destroy and create life.

Learning to control fire gave humans the means to transform their diet, master the environment and conquer new territories. Fire is warmth, protection and safety. It has allowed us to make tools and pottery, smelt metal and generate power. We cook, we cleanse, we purify with fire.

Fire is both a warning and a welcome; it can scare away animals or invite social interaction. Fire is light, heat, smoke and steam, the very building blocks of the Industrial Revolution.

But fire is also intimate. It's the tool we use to keep our loved ones warm. It represents home, hearth and belonging. We use it to celebrate, cohere and commemorate. We build fires for fun, for pleasure, for a break from our over-engineered lives. For all our access to technology, it seems nothing can sever our ancient ties with fire.

Throughout civilisation, people have been fascinated and frightened by fire in equal measure – we use it, but we innately understand that we never truly control it. It's both lifesaver and destroyer in one. And, as humans are wont to do, what we both fear and revere we transform into something mystical. Throughout the world and history, fire has taken on deep symbolic meaning – from the phoenix in Greek mythology, who rises from the ashes to symbolize renewal and rebirth, to Vesta, the Roman fire goddess of hearth and home – many cultures have worshipped flames as a force for good. Even today, we talk of smouldering desire and hearts on fire. Love is an eternal flame; we long for someone to 'light our fire'. Fire is passion, courage and energy.

But fire also scares us. We talk of fiery hells and raging infernos. People who metaphorically 'play with fire' almost always get burned. Fire is fury, anger, burning hatred. We advise people against 'fanning the fire' or 'going down in flames'. Who wants a friend with a fiery temper or hot head? Fire is death, apocalypse, destruction. Perhaps that's why fire still has such a hold over us. We have mastered so much of our world, perhaps it does us good to have something we can't quite dominate. Fire brings us so much pleasure and comfort, but it can also thwart us and test our abilities. As Alan Bennett writes in *The Madness of George III*, 'To be curbed, stood up to, in a word, thwarted, exercises the character, elasticates the spirit, makes it more pliant.' In other words, a little bit of a challenge is no bad thing.

Fire Now

Simple pleasures are making a comeback: sleeping under the stars, baking bread, crafting and potting just for sheer creative delight of it. Fires are just a natural extension of this rediscovery. There's so much that's better about modern-day living – health, life expectancy, social mobility – and yet our genetic memory sometimes beckons us back; we feel a longing for the satisfaction that comes from performing basic, life-sustaining tasks. Gathering, chopping and setting light to your own fire gives you a sense of achievement that's difficult to rival. In a world of confusing technology and breakneck change, there's no doubt that firecraft makes you feel *accomplished* in a tangible, practical way.

Sitting next to a log fire, watching the flames flicker, is as close to meditation as many of us get. When we experience a roaring fire, all our senses are absorbed – this calming focus of attention takes us away from our quotidian worries, soothes our anxieties and pulls us close. It's an unconscious response, an embedded memory that reminds us that at one time fire meant heat, protection and, above all, community. In other words, we have *evolved* to enjoy being around fires – for thousands of years, the act of building and burning a fire was the most important means of encouraging social cohesion. We may not need fire in the same critical way as our ancestors, but few would deny that the quiet, reassuring pleasure that comes from flames is as welcome as it's always been.

Fire and Nature

One of the magical side-effects of learning to build a fire is the knowledge and connection it gives you to nature. From working out which twigs burn best to gauging wind direction, there's a strong case to be made for picking up or dusting off some Baden-Powell basics.

You don't have to know about wine to get pleasure from it. Equally, you don't have to appreciate nature to enjoy an open fire. But gaining expertise on the types of wood that burn, the effect of weather on flames or how to find free kindling in the forest adds immensely to the enjoyment of open fires. The act of gathering kindling and firewood brings you into contact with aspects of nature you might not have noticed or even thought about. The forest becomes a store cupboard of ingredients – you'll never look at cedar bark, pine cones, dry grass, catkins or dried old birds' nests in the same way again. Handle enough wood and you'll soon learn to appreciate the satisfying snap of a well-seasoned twig, or

what it means when bark peels easily away in your hand.

Building fires is fun. But it's also profound. Most of us live a life divorced from our natural surroundings. By understanding and engaging with the natural world – whether it's hunting for sticks on a woodland walk or raking the ashes into the vegetable plot – we develop a greater respect for the environment and a real sense of self-sufficiency. Get children involved and you open up a whole new world where they can build, create and feel confidently free in their wild surroundings.

Fire and Survival

If you live in the countryside, power cuts are all too common, especially during bad weather or when the in-laws are just about to arrive. It's not unusual to be left without electricity for hours, so having at least one open fire or wood burner in your home means you'll never be cold, and you'll have the wherewithal to toast crumpets, bake a jacket potato or heat water until the power returns.

Knowing how to build a fire also comes in very handy if you're keen on camping, hiking or any kind of adventuring on the road less travelled. It's surprising how many people get lost, injured or disorientated on wilderness trips. If you're an active, outdoors person, firecraft is a useful string to your bow; a fire can be used to signal for assistance, boost morale, cook food and keep you warm until help arrives. There's also a psychological benefit – the can-do frame of mind that comes from knowing some basic survival skills has been shown time and time again to improve the likelihood of a good outcome if you ever find yourself in a sticky situation.

This isn't a survival manual, and there are lots of really good courses and reads on the subject. What this book *will* give you is a better understanding of how fire burns, what it needs to thrive, how to create sparks and what makes good fuel – all snippets which could just come in handy in a crisis. A little knowledge isn't always a dangerous thing.

Fire and Cooking

On a camping trip, the evening meal, cooked over an open fire, is the highlight of the day. There's a level of skill involved in campfire cooking that requires total concentration – the fire is a living, changing creature, and you have to respond quickly to its moods or the food will spoil.

But there's also an elegant simplicity to it – some of the best meals you can cook on a fire are those with just a handful of ingredients. There are few things more delicious than a pan-fried rib-eye served with fresh herbs, or a buttered corn-on-the-cob baked in the dying embers. The fire, smoke and open surroundings imbue the food with an inimitable flavour and a sense of occasion that you just don't get from conventional cooking. Building and managing a cooking fire takes knowledge and proficiency. Transforming raw ingredients into a hearty meal needs patience and intuition. Food that's quickly prepared and convenient often isn't appreciated; food that has taken time and skill to create is always more satisfying.

Many of us as young kids will have enjoyed the feeling of independence and maturity that came with campfire cooking. We might not have been allowed in the kitchen, but we could certainly rustle up a feast of marshmallows, toast and hot chocolate without any pesky adults getting involved. From school residentials to family camping trips, backyard adventures to Girl Guide outings, many of our happiest memories involve cooking over fire. If, as an adult, you can recapture even just a fragment of those first experiences, that's got to be something worth cherishing.

Fire and The Environment

The debate about timber as an eco-fuel smoulders on, and it can be tricky to know if you are doing the right thing in turning back to wood. It's complex, but in essence, as a tree grows, it absorbs carbon dioxide from the air. When that same tree burns or rots, it releases the same amount of CO_2 back into the atmosphere. So, whether you leave a tree to decompose on the forest floor or set fire to it, the same amount of carbon is released back into the air. In other words, wood is carbon-neutral. If we chop down trees, we can also plant more. Coal and gas are both finite.

The problem comes with processing and transporting timber to your doorstep. Industrial logging, lorries and petrol-fuelled chainsaws all push up timber's carbon footprint. Added to that, when wood burns at a low temperature it releases smoke that contains small amounts of harmful pollutants, called particulates. Wood fires, it seems, aren't always as ecologically friendly as we would hope.

So, what's the answer? If you follow a BUY RIGHT, BURN RIGHT philosophy, there are few fuels that can match timber for eco-credentials, especially when we combine our ancient knowledge of seasoning with new, efficient wood-burning stoves:

- Gather your own wood or buy from a local supplier.

- Dry wood burns hotter and cleaner than wet wood – only use seasoned timber.

- An open fire burns four logs for every one in a wood burner. Use wood-burning stoves for everyday heat and open fires for special occasions.

- If you live in a smoke control area, stick to authorized fuels such as briquettes and/or an exempt wood burner.

- Don't burn rubbish, treated timber or plastics on your fire.

- Buy the smallest wood-burning stove you need – 5 kilowatts is plenty for a normal-sized living room.

- Look for ways to improve your home's thermal efficiency. Better insulation equals less fuel needed.

Fire and Cost

How does wood stack up financially when compared to other ways to heat your home? As a general rule (although prices do fluctuate), of the three standard ways to heat your home, mains gas is cheapest; oil is next, with LPG (liquefied petroleum gas) and electric heating the most expensive. On a like-for-like basis, biomass (e.g. wood pellets, chips and logs) is somewhere in the middle.

Few people heat their homes exclusively with wood – unless they have a biomass boiler – so for most people, the issue is whether wood is good value as a secondary source of heating. As a rough guide, if you plan to use an average 5kW wood burner for moderate use (e.g. weekends and evenings), you'll probably need about 3–4 cubic metres (105–140 ft³) of seasoned logs over the burning season (October–March). For intensive use – morning, day and evening – you can double that to 6–8 cubic metres (211–282 ft³). The general consensus is that running one wood-burning stove will knock about 10% off the average household fuel bill, and in many cases more, especially if you have the space to store and dry cheaper, unseasoned logs.

The economics don't stack up quite as well when logs are expensive to source (such as in large urban areas), you don't have room to store wood and so can't save money by buying in bulk, or you want to heat a home with an open fire, which burns less efficiently than a wood burner. For many people, however, the choice to enjoy a crackling fire isn't primarily about cost. It's about the things money can't buy.

Fire and Fun

If your house is well served by central heating it begs the question: why have a wood fire at all? The pleasure of a real fire is difficult to unpick – part of the satisfaction lies in creating something from nothing; other times it's the welcome distraction that comes from focusing on a practical task. But sometimes, the reason to build a fire is just because it's fun. Not 'fun' in the vacuous, commercial sense of the word, but fun in its truest form. It's genuinely life-affirming to gather in a field with friends and welcome in the stars around a roaring campfire; it's delicious to cook a freshly caught mackerel on a beach or share a winter's evening toasting muffins with your offspring, who are still little enough to be impressed by your ability to make flames spring to life.

Part of the thrill of being on holiday, whether it's camping in the countryside or hiring a cosy cottage, is that it gives us the chance to exercise our primitive fire-making muscles. We know we don't *need* firecraft in the same way that our ancestors did, but we certainly seem to relish the opportunity to practise it. Fire is also part of our celebratory consciousness. From bonfires to fireworks, barbeques to birthday candles, it seems a party just isn't a party without a few sparks.

CHAPTER TWO

The Anatomy of Fire

'The mind is not a vessel to be filled,
but a fire to be kindled.'

PLUTARCH

How Fire Works

Fire isn't a thing. It's a chemical reaction. And one that needs three things to work – fuel, oxygen and a source of heat. Remove any one of these three things and the fire goes out. In the case of a wood fire, the fuel is the kindling and logs, the oxygen comes from the surrounding air and the heat comes initially from the flame of a match.

But what happens then? How does wood burn, and what is being released? It's helpful to think of a wood fire having three stages:

The first stage – when the fire is first lit, the logs release volatile gases and burn off any water vapour. You won't get much heat at this stage, just smoke and steam. You want to get through this stage as quickly as possible, which is why you need dry, not wet, wood.

The second stage – when the fire really takes hold, the volatile gases start to ignite into flames and produce heat. The flames, in turn, ignite more of the logs and release more volatile gases, and the fire becomes self-perpetuating.

The third stage – once the fire is really hot, and the wood has burned off all its volatile gases, you are left with char and ash. Char is almost entirely carbon and glows red hot, giving off plenty of heat without any smoke or flames. Once the fire has died out, all that's left is the ash (all the unburnable minerals from the wood, such as calcium carbonate, phosphate and potash), which just happens to be brilliant for your garden (see Ashes, page 154).

Heat

Open fires, campfires and wood-burning stoves all emit heat. But did you know that they warm you up in different ways?

With a wood-burning stove, heat is transferred into your living room mostly by conduction (the metal body of the stove gets very hot) and radiation (the fire emits electromagnetic waves of heat and light). What wood burners are traditionally not so good at is convection, making hot air rise and circulate around the room.

Open fires, on the other hand, mostly rely on radiation and convection to heat the room but, because they are not encased in a metal stove, don't get much chance to conduct heat. Knowing this, there are a few things you can do to improve either's performance. If you've got a wood-burning stove, try a stove fan to improve convection. These nifty devices push warm air around the room using power generated from the heat of the stove. Or if you've got an open fire, look into ways of introducing a metal insert, surround or fireback to the hearth, all of which will conduct heat or bounce it back into the room. As both types of fire radiate heat, it's also a good idea not to put too many obstacles – such as armchairs or high-sided ottomans that will block the heat – between you and the fireplace.

Outdoor fires are different again. There's no metal to conduct any heat, and all the warm convected air billows straight upwards into the night sky, so campfires rely almost solely on radiation to warm you up. That explains why your cheeks are always hot while your bum gets cold. One solution is to build a 'reflector' next to your campfire (see Which Fire to Build, page 136).

Firelight

We know that fire is a chemical reaction that produces heat. What we often miss, however, is the notion that fire produces another useful by-product – light.

When you are planning a lighting scheme for a room, spare a thought for firelight. General (or ambient) lighting provides the overall illumination for the room, and task lighting, such as reading light, is useful for focusing in on specific activities. But there's another type of lighting – decorative or accent lighting – whose sole purpose is to draw attention to a specific area or object, or to be a feature in itself. Flames are nature's fairy lights – decorative lighting at its most captivating.

Firelight is a magical experience, a kinetic, dancing light that captures your gaze and provides endless opportunity for focus and reflection, especially in the dark. Firelight flickers and bounces off reflective surfaces; it also casts a gentle orange glow over everything it touches. With this in mind, if you are going to enjoy an open fire, resist the urge to over-illuminate the rest of the room or you'll kill the effect. An over-bright room will strip the fire of all its cosy potential and take away its power as a focal point. Forget spotlights and overhead pendants; embrace low, subtle lighting – such as table lamps and picture lights – and make your fire the star of the show.

Combustion

We already know that fire goes through different stages. Once it's lit, the fire goes through the 'flaming combustion' stage, when all the wood's volatile gases are burned as flames. Only once this stage has completed can the fire move on to the 'glowing combustion' stage, when it burns as hot, glowing embers. Each stage is useful for different things – the flaming stage produces lots of light and quick heat, while the glowing stage is hotter, flameless and more stable to cook on.

The kind of wood you use can actually help your fire reach its various stages more quickly or prolong them, depending on what you want. As a general rule, softwoods like pine, larch, redwood and cedar are less dense than hardwoods and tend to burn quick and short. That makes them easier to light, good for kindling, and the ideal wood for producing lots of flames. Softwoods are also cheaper and season more quickly (see Does All Wood Burn?, page 68) but have a tendency to leave resin tar residues on the inside of your chimney.

Hardwoods, on the other hand, tend to be dense and are better for putting out sustained heat over a longer period of time. They also burn down to a hot bed of embers, ideal for cooking over. Hardwoods are more expensive (because they take longer to grow) but burn more cleanly. Regardless of type, the drier and smaller the wood, the quicker it will light and burn.

Wood Burners

With open fires, about three-quarters of the heat is wasted up the chimney. With wood-burning stoves, more than three-quarters of the heat stays in the room. This difference has a huge bearing on how many logs you need to burn on each type of fire and therefore how expensive, relatively, they are to run.

For those of us deciding whether to buy a wood burner, however, the economics are slightly more complex, as you'll need to factor in the cost of a stove and professional installation. Estimates suggest that the payback period is between about five and ten years, depending on how much you use the stove.

Wood burners also combust wood in a different way to open fires – modern stoves recirculate air through the stove, which not only makes them combust more efficiently but also means that most of the harmful particulates and gases burn off before they reach the chimney. Many homes in towns and cities are within smoke control areas, where you can't emit smoke from a chimney unless you're burning an authorized fuel (see Briquettes, page 85) or using an exempt appliance. Most modern wood burners are classed as exempt.

One thing the open fire has over the wood-burning stove, however, is the sensory experience. Tucked behind a glass door, the stove fire is safer, less smoky but also silent, more removed. Wood burners don't work well with their doors open, so if you want a fire for its delightful crackle, or for toasting crumpets or making scented smoke, best to stick to the traditional hearth.

Banking Up

Some people recommend stuffing your wood-burning stove with enough fuel to keep it going through the night until morning. This is called 'banking up', and while this idea sounds good in principle – how cosy to wake up to a still-glowing fire – in practice it's actually bad news for your wood burner and potentially lethal.

Modern wood-burning stoves are designed to burn efficiently by operating at a high temperature, with plenty of airflow and properly seasoned logs. All the methods people use to bank up their wood burner at night affect the efficiency of this combustion. One traditional trick, for example, is to light unseasoned logs, the idea being that the wet wood burns at a low, smouldering temperature for longer. This might make the fire last a few more hours, but it leads to condensation and other acidic residues that can damage your flue and the inside of the stove.

Other techniques, like restricting the airflow or filling the stove to the brim, result in the fire not being able to get hot enough to combust fully – not a good idea, especially when it can result in the production of the lethal gas carbon monoxide.

One absolute no-no is adding coal. While you can buy multi-fuel stoves (see page 88), wood-burning stoves are designed to burn timber exclusively. Wood burns best on a flat bed of ash, whereas coal needs to sit on a raised grate to allow extra airflow. Burning coal and wood together in a wood burner will mean neither combust properly, leaving sulphuric acid deposits to corrode your flue, and you run the risk of damaging your stove or, even worse, causing a flue gas explosion in the stove or chimney.

Chimneys

If a fire is the heart of the house, the chimney is the lungs. Its sole purpose in life is to help the air in your home stay breathable and allow harmful flue gases to escape up and out of the roof.

If you are new to a property and don't know whether the chimney works, *don't use it* until it's been smoke-tested and swept (see Sweeps, page 184). Even if you know the fireplace works, if you are putting an old chimney back into use after a long period of disuse, it'll need testing and sweeping. Chimneys have a habit of getting blocked by nests, animals, debris and smoky residues, all of which can restrict airflow or cause a chimney fire.

If you're fitting a wood-burning stove into an existing chimney, it will need a metal flue liner. This is for three reasons: wood burns at a lower temperature than coal, and therefore harmful deposits such as tar are more likely to stick to the inside of the chimney; a metal liner will stop noxious fumes such as carbon monoxide leaking into upstairs rooms; and a metal liner keeps the flue gases warmer for longer, helping them rise up and out of the chimney. The stove manufacturer can tell you the specific size you need.

If your property does not have a chimney, an insulated metal flue can be installed. These can look handsomely architectural and, because they are lined, aren't dangerously hot to the touch.

Air

If you try to burn a fire where there's not enough oxygen – in a sealed room, for example – instead of carbon dioxide, you get carbon monoxide, an odourless, colourless gas that's the most common cause of fatal poisoning. That's why if you want a wood fire in your home, whether it's an open fire or a wood burner, you must ensure there's a constant supply of fresh air.

Most old homes were so draughty that open fires had a ready supply of oxygen, whether it came from leaky windows or howling floorboards. Fresh air could be drawn from both outside and other rooms in the house, helping the fire burn efficiently. In the modern home, which puts a greater emphasis on draught reduction and insulation, many of these sources of air are now blocked.

It's not practical to have a window open all the time, especially when you're trying to keep warm, which is why building regulations insist that any fires that take their combustion air from within the home must have a ventilator that is fixed permanently open to provide fresh air from outside. It's not a difficult job to fit one, and it's absolutely essential – not only is it a legal issue, it's a lifesaver.

If you are buying a wood-burning stove from a HETAS-approved company (see Directory, page 202), they will be able to give you guidance about ventilation. If you have an existing wood-burning stove or open fire, take advice from a HETAS engineer about whether there is adequate ventilation in the room.

How to Put Out a Fire

So, you've got your fire going, but how do you put it out? Firstly, stop putting any more fuel on the fire at least an hour before you want it to stop. If you have a wood-burning stove, simply make sure the glass door is tightly closed and the primary air vent is shut (this is usually the vent at the bottom of the stove). The secondary air vent stays open – this allows the stove to keep burning at a safe level of combustion while slowly dying out. Never throw water on a wood-burning stove; it could crack the cast metal.

With an open fire, kill it in two stages. Stage one – take a poker and 'open up' the fire by separating any burning logs. Gently spread out the embers; this will cool the fire. Stage two – use a spray bottle to lightly spritz the flames with water. Don't flood the fire; it makes the ashes sticky and fills the room with smoke. A sprinkling of sand or cold ashes will do the same trick (you'll need to clear out the sand before you make a new fire). Even if the fire looks dead, ALWAYS put a fireguard up before you leave the room – it only takes one stray spark.

To put out a campfire, it's the same principle. Use a stick or metal shovel to separate the logs and flatten out the embers. Pour water over the hot ashes until the hissing stops. If you don't have any water, stir soil or sand into the embers to smother the flames. Never bury a fire; it can smoulder for hours.

CHAPTER THREE

Finding Firewood

'Beechwood fires burn bright and clear,
Hornbeam blazes too,
If the logs are kept a year, to season
through and through.

Oaken logs will warm you well, if they're
old and dry,
Larch logs of pinewood smell but the
sparks will fly.

Pine is good and so is Yew for warmth
through wintry days,
The Poplar and the Willow too, they take
too long to blaze.'

OLD ENGLISH FOLK SONG

Does All Wood Burn?

The short answer is yes. The longer, honest answer is that some woods burn better than others. When we're thinking of firewood, it's helpful to divide timber into two kinds – softwood and hardwood. The names don't refer to the texture of the wood – some hardwoods are soft and vice versa.

Softwoods come from conifer trees, which are evergreen, needle-leaved and have cones – fir and pine are both good examples.

Hardwoods come from broad-leaved deciduous trees – species like oak, elm, ash and cherry fall into this category.

So which to burn? As a general rule, hardwoods are denser than softwood so provide a longer burn. They also have less resin than softwood, so they are not as prone to clog up your chimney with tar. Hardwood is, however, more difficult to ignite, so you'll find that most kindling is made from softwood.

GOOD TO BURN	SKIP IT
Wooden pallets, cable drums and crates (don't burn if stamped 'MB' as this means it has been treated with methyl bromide, a fumigant. 'HB' means heat-treated so is fine to burn.)	Sheet materials (chipboard, melamine, veneers, hardboard, plywood, MDF, OSB board)
Untreated framing and studwork timber	Laminate and engineered flooring
Planed softwood and hardwood	Painted or varnished wood
Solid wood flooring and skirting boards (unvarnished/unpainted)	Outdoor timber (decking, cladding, cedar shingles, site pegs, gates, fences and posts)
Scaffold boards (untreated)	Salvaged sleepers and telegraph poles
Thermowood	Sheds and summerhouses
Untreated shiplap or tongue and groove	Roofing battens
Roofing trusses	

You can burn a fire entirely with softwood, but because it doesn't last as long as hardwood, you'll find yourself throwing on logs at an alarming rate. Softwood also tends to spit and smoke, which can be tricky for an open fire.

Softwood does have the advantage of being cheaper than hardwood – this is because it seasons more quickly (see Seasoning, page 104), it's readily available and you get less heat output per log than hardwood.

So what's the solution? Most people find a workable compromise and burn a mix of the two. Softwood will bring heat quickly and cheaply, while hardwood burns slow and long. Think of softwood as the sprinter fuel and hardwood as the distance runner.

It's worth noting that wood-burning stoves are less fussy about what they will burn as the combustion process is more efficient. That said, the more softwood you burn, the more often you'll need to have your chimney swept.

Tree Table

	Firewood quality	Aromatic smoke	Seasoning time	Green burning	Comments
Apple	**Good**	✓	1-2 years		Burns well with plenty of heat and no sparking. Sweetly fragranced smoke.
Ash	**Excellent**	✓	1 year	✓	Burns well with plenty of heat and flames and no sparking. Splits easily with an axe.
Beech	**Excellent**		1-2 years		Burns well with few sparks. Needs a long seasoning. Good for embers.
Birch	**Very Good**	✓	1 year	✓	Burns well but fast. Best mixed with a slower fuel such as oak. Bark is great for tinder and kindling.
Cedar	**Very Good**	✓	6-12 months	✓	Burns well but fast. Deliciously fragranced smoke. Can green-burn small pieces.
Cherry	**Good**	✓	1-2 years		Burns well with few sparks. Sweetly fragranced smoke.
Elm	**Excellent**	✓	2 years		Good, lasting heat and burns slowly. Not too many sparks. Needs a long seasoning.
Eucalyptus	**Good**	✓	1 year		Burns fast with a pleasantly fragrant smoke - not too many sparks.
Hawthorn	**Very Good**		1-2 years		Not readily available as a firewood but burns slow and hot with few sparks.
Hazel	**Very Good**	✓	1 year		Not readily available as a firewood but burns fast without many sparks.

	Firewood quality	Aromatic smoke	Seasoning time	Green burning	Comments
lly	**Good**		1 year	✓	A fast-burning, moderate-heat firewood that can be burned green if necessary.
rnbeam	**Excellent**		2 years		Burns well. Not many sparks. Excellent embers.
rse estnut	**Poor**		1–2 years		Burns moderately to poorly. Difficult to split. Unpleasant-smelling smoke.
rch	**Good**		1 year		Sooty and prone to sparks but burns quite well.
me	**Poor**		1 year		Burns poorly. Unpleasant-smelling smoke.
ak	**Excellent**	✓	2 years		One of the best firewoods. Gives off a good, lasting heat and burns slow and hot. Produces lots of ash.
ar	**Good**	✓	1–2 years		Burns well. No sparking or spitting. Sweetly fragranced smoke.
ne	**Good**	✓	1 year		Sooty and prone to sparks but good for kindling.
wan	**Good**		1–2 years		Burns well and reasonably slowly.
ruce	**Good**	✓	1 year		Low quality but fine for kindling.
weet hestnut	**Good**		1–2 years		Prone to excessive sparks. Not for use on an open fire but burns well.
aple (inc. ycamore)	**Good**	✓	6–12 months	✓	Burns quite hot with plenty of flames. Not prone to sparks.
alnut	**Good**	✓	1 year		Burns well but quite quickly. Lovely-smelling smoke.

Wood That's No Good

Just because you can set fire to something doesn't mean you should. Here's what not to burn:

Treated Timber – Preservatives, fungicides, creosote, paints, glues, varnishes and other chemical additives can release highly toxic fumes and will damage your chimney. Steer clear of burning MDF, chipboard, plywood, decking, stained, tanalized or painted timber and anything treated for outdoor use. SOLUTION? Recycle it instead.

Non-Local Timber – Never move firewood long distances. Transporting logs around the country can spread invasive species, tree pests and fungi that cause diseases such as ash dieback and pine needle blight – threatening woodland and native species. SOLUTION? Buy it where you burn it.

Green Timber – Unless it's an emergency, avoid burning wet or unseasoned wood. It's not only hard to light, but it also burns inefficiently, pollutes the atmosphere with particulates and clogs up your chimney. SOLUTION? Season it properly (see Seasoning, page 104).

Poisonous Timber – There's scant research into tree species and toxic smoke, so local knowledge and folklore are often all we have to rely on. Traditionally, oleander, poison ivy, poison oak and sumac are cited as being very poisonous to inhale. SOLUTION? Only burn timber listed in the Tree Table (page 72).

Driftwood – While it burns well, salt-laden driftwood produces smoke that can speed up the corrosion of metal stoves and flue parts. Recent research also suggests that burning sodium chloride releases toxic dioxins at high temperatures. SOLUTION? Avoid if possible.

Buying Firewood

You can only compare like with like, so if you want to find a reputable, fairly priced supply of firewood, you need to know what you should be asking for:

Volume Not Weight – Buy wood by volume *not* weight; that way you won't be fobbed off with heavy, unseasoned logs. Ask what you are getting in cubic metres – suppliers often sell by the trailer-load or bag, but they need to clarify what that equates to in volume. If they won't tell you, go elsewhere. You wouldn't order other heating fuels without knowing exactly how much you were getting.

Softwood or Hardwood – Is the seller offering softwood or hardwood? Hardwood costs more for the same volume of softwood but will last longer. Do you want just hardwood or a mix of the two?

Green or Seasoned – You can buy green (freshly cut), part-seasoned or fully seasoned logs. Green is cheapest, but you will have to season it before you burn it. If you have the space and plan months ahead, this can be cost-efficient. If you want to burn it now, buy fully seasoned. Invest in a moisture meter so you can check any deliveries (see Moisture Meters, page 106). Kiln-dried logs (see page 83) are another alternative.

Sustainable Sources – Only choose firewood from a sustainable, ethical source. Foreign imports of logs have heavy carbon footprints, and it can be difficult to find out whether the producer is committed to responsible, sustainable woodland management. Look out for quality assurance schemes such as Woodsure or buy from a locally managed estate.

Scavenging

It's actually trickier to scavenge wood than you think. Most woodland is privately owned and managed, whether it's by a forestry organisation or a landowner, and the trees – alive or dead – are their property. Taking wood to burn without permission is effectively theft. That said, there are ways of collecting wood in the wild:

Scavenging Permits – You might be able to apply for a scavenging licence from your local forestry commission or group. This usually involves paying a small fee in exchange for access to a site for a short period to collect the leftovers from a major forestry felling operation.

Local Landowners – Some woodland owners may be happy for you to remove deadwood or take part in thinning or coppicing days in return for a portion of the rewards. It's worth starting a dialogue with the local landowner to see if there's any labour you could volunteer in return for firewood.

Estover Rights – People, known as 'commoners', are entitled to use 'common land' land or take resources from it. Estover rights allow commoners to take timber, such as whole trees or firewood. In practice, these ancient rights are rare, but your property's title deeds or a solicitor can tell you more.

Grow Your Own – If you have land, there may be grants and funding available to help you create your own copse or woodland. Even a largish garden can support enough trees for a modest firewood supply – choose quick-growing hardwood varieties that produce good-quality firewood, such as alder, ash, hawthorn and sycamore.

Salvage

A vast amount of wood is sent to landfill each year, much of it burnable. One of the issues is knowing what's safe to burn and what's best left for the skip. Anything that's engineered, laminated, treated or painted will contain glues, formaldehyde, fungicides or other chemicals that are harmful to humans if burned. Most scrap is softwood, so best kept for kindling or to mix with hardwood on an open fire. A wood burner will cope admirably with softwood, but remember, you'll need to sweep your chimney more often.

Kiln-dried Logs

For a fire to burn effectively and cleanly, logs need to be no more than 25% water, and ideally less than that (see Seasoning, page 104). The traditional way to get to this point is to dry or 'season' your wood for a long period of time, how long will depend on the species. If you haven't got the space to store wet logs, need dry wood in a hurry, or want the guarantee that your timber is fully seasoned, you can pay a premium and buy kiln-dried logs.

As the name suggests, logs are 'cooked' in a large kiln to quicken the process of drying. In many cases, kiln-dried logs are actually drier than seasoned logs (typically between 10% and 20%), which makes them popular for a number of reasons. The lack of moisture means a cleaner, hotter burn than traditionally seasoned logs, so people find they use fewer kiln-dried logs to get the same heat output, which may help offset the higher price. The hotter burn also creates fewer particulates, which is good news for air quality and your chimney.

Whether kiln-dried logs are universally better for the environment is more difficult to calculate, as fuel is also needed to heat the kilns. Many kiln-dried logs also travel large distances, adding significantly to their carbon footprint, and may come from forests which aren't sustainably managed. If you can find a supplier who uses waste wood, renewable energy or biomass to heat their kilns and sources their wood from local, managed woodland, you've got the best of both worlds. Look for the Woodsure logo.

Briquettes

What looks like a log, burns like a log, but isn't a log? The answer? A briquette.

Briquettes/Heat Logs – Created from compressed sawdust, briquettes have the benefit of burning hotter and cleaner than traditional logs and taking up half the space. They also score eco-points for using up a waste product of the timber industry. Briquettes don't have quite the same aesthetic appeal of logs, nor the fragrant smoke, but if you're using a wood burner this doesn't matter so much.

Brackettes – Brackettes are made from bracken that has been shredded and compressed into blocks. They are eco-friendly, mainly because the harvesting process increases biodiversity, and burn hotter and longer than oak. Brackettes work best on a hot, well-established fire and burn with a pleasant moorland aroma.

Coffee Logs™ – Another carbon-neutral bio-fuel, Coffee Logs use up spent coffee grounds. They burn hotter and longer than wood, but are too hot for a wood-burning stove, so should be used on open fires and multi-fuel stoves only.

DIY Paper Logs – Making paper logs may seem like a handy way of using up old newspapers, but it's not so good for your chimney or local air quality. While black ink burns fairly cleanly, coloured ink, which is used in most newspapers produces noxious fumes and particulates that contribute to air pollution and flue damage.

Charcoal – NEVER use charcoal on an indoor fire or wood-burning stove. It releases significant amounts of poisonous carbon monoxide (even after it starts to cool down). Charcoal also burns too hot for a wood-burning stove.

Coal

Lots of people burn wood and coal together, but it's not always a good idea.

Wood and coal burn differently – Wood needs to burn on a flat surface with an air supply from above. Coal needs air from *underneath,* so sits on a raised grate. The grate also allows coal ash to escape without blocking the air supply. While wood and coal will burn together, you won't be getting the maximum efficiency from either.

Wood and coal create sulphuric acid – Burning wood and coal together risks causing serious damage to your chimney or flue. Wood contains water. Coal contains sulphur. Burn them simultaneously and you create sulphuric acid, which is corrosive and could shorten the life of your stove or chimney. Using a handful of seasoned kindling to start a coal fire isn't an issue; it's burning the two fuels together over a prolonged period that can cause problems.

Coal will kill your wood-burning stove – Coal burns at a much hotter temperature than timber. The materials used to make many wood-burning stoves are simply not designed to take repeated and long-standing exposure to extreme temperatures and may warp or crack.

Multi-fuel stoves – Multi-fuel stoves are designed to be able to adapt to different types of fuel, either by including a removable grate or having different options for air supply. If you want to switch between fuels, these can be a good option, but most manufacturers will still recommend that you don't mix fuels in the same fire.

CHAPTER FOUR

Chop, Stack, Store

'To love is to burn, to be on fire.'

JANE AUSTEN, *Sense and Sensibility*

Chopping Blocks

While some people choose to split wood directly on the floor, there are three good reasons to use a block. Firstly, it's safer – you want the axe to land well away from your feet; secondly, it's easier on your back – you don't have to bring the axe down beyond knee height; and finally, it reduces the chances of your axe being damaged through hitting the ground or bouncing off any stray rocks. Beyond that, there are some common-sense rules behind choosing your chop-spot:

- Find somewhere well away from windows, animals and other people, and give yourself plenty of room to swing the axe.

- To prevent double handling, see if you can split the logs next to where you plan to stack them.

- Always set your block to face the approach – you don't want people walking up behind you unheard or unseen.

- Find a good chopping block. A cut tree stump or section of trunk is ideal. You can find chopping blocks online if you can't source one locally.

- Choose a block that is wide, heavy, flat on both ends, and right for your height – the axe should strike the end of the log at a right angle. Most people find a comfortable height and width is about 35 centimetres (14 in) by 35 centimetres.

- Sit the block on solid, stable ground. If you place a chopping block on a soft surface such as a lawn, you'll find much of the energy is absorbed into the ground.

- The block must be absolutely stable. If it's wobbly, a glancing blow could hit your lower body or send the timber flying off.

Splitting Wood

1. *Choose your weapon.* You'll need either a splitting axe or a maul (a cross between a heavy axe and a sledgehammer). For most small logs, a splitting axe is fine.

2. *Wear the right clothes.* Wear safety glasses, gloves to prevent blisters, and solid work boots (preferably steel toed).

3. *Stand correctly.* Stand squarely facing your chopping block, feet shoulder-width apart. Don't stand with one leg in front of the other – if you miss your front leg is the first place an axe will land.

4. *Choose your log.* You need straight sections of timber that will balance upright when placed on the chopping block. Don't attempt to split curved logs or ones with large knots – you'll be endlessly thwarted.

5. *Read the wood.* Exploit any existing cracks or splits. Failing that, aim for the centre.

6. *Hold the axe properly.* Hold the base of the handle in one hand (most people prefer their left hand). Slide your right hand up the shaft to near the head of the axe.

7. *Use one motion.* In a single fluid action, raise the axe over your shoulder. Letting the weight of the axe do the work, bring the axe down onto the log, letting your right hand slide down the shaft to meet the left.

8. *Let the axe do the work.* Allow the momentum and sheer weight of the axe to provide the muscle power, not your own brute force. You are simply guiding the axe to where it needs to fall.

The Perfect Log Store

A log store should do two things: help the seasoning process, and protect your firewood from the elements. If you want to build one or buy one, bear a few things in mind:

Breathability – Any design must allow air to circulate. This helps the logs dry out, ready for burning. That's why so many log stores have slatted or open sides.

Stability – A sizeable stack of logs will exert significant pressure on the sides and base of your log store. The ground needs to be stable and level.

Airflow – Air needs to flow underneath the log store, so the base should be slightly raised off the ground (on feet or bearers). A gravel or hardstanding surface is better than grass or soil.

Weather – Try not to site your log store where it will catch the prevailing bad weather. A sunny, airy spot that isn't vulnerable to driving rain is ideal.

Walls – If you want to put your logs next to a wall, leave an air gap of 5 centimetres (2 in).

This aids the drying process and stops moisture penetrating the bricks.

Materials – Most timber won't hold up to weather without treatment. Buy outdoor-grade timber or species that naturally resist decay, such as oak and cedar. Any nails or fixings need to be rust-resistant.

Size – Estimate how many cubic metres of logs you'll need a year (see Fire and Cost, page 38) and aim to stack a year's worth. If you want to season your own green wood (see Seasoning, page 104), ideally you should have three separate stores or areas – one for fully seasoned (two years old), one for part-seasoned (one year) and one for green (this year's). Or, if you use seasoned logs, you can store less and buy more often.

How to Stack Logs

Few things are more pleasing than a neatly stacked log pile. It's not just a thing of beauty; it's the larder for your fire, so you need to be able to grab the right mix of ingredients in one go.

Logs should be uniform lengths – Cut or buy the right size log for your fire or wood burner – usually around 30 centimetres (12 in) (the length of a school ruler).

Don't have logs too chunky – Wood should be split to a variety of sizes, ranging from 7 to 15 centimetres (3 to 6 in) measured at its widest point.

Split is always best – The extra surface area speeds up the seasoning process.

Think in horizontal lines – Plan to stack and remove logs in lines, rather than working randomly through the pile.

Mix sizes across the lines – You'll use a variety of different-sized logs in the course of a fire, so stack each horizontal line with a mix of large and small logs.

Don't try and pack too tightly – Build in air gaps to help the drying process – mixing up the sizes of logs helps with this.

Place bark upwards – Logs should be stacked bark side up as this will help the firewood shed any moisture that comes in from above.

Keep it stable – Don't take from the middle or bottom of the pile; it'll destabilize the stack. If you want to stack more than one log deep, use a double length log to bridge both stacks and create a 'tie' between the two.

Keep kindling separately – A large bin or box is ideal for kindling, which just needs to be kept dry and easily accessible.

Green Wood

When you cut a tree down, the freshly felled wood is about 50% moisture. That means every unseasoned log you throw on a fire is half timber, half water. A fire must drive off this water before it can start to kick out any decent heat, so by using wet wood you are radically slowing down the rate at which your room will warm up.

If a fire burns too coolly, it also doesn't burn as cleanly. Setting fire to unseasoned wood means that harmful particulates and gases don't burn off before they reach the chimney – not great for the environment or your air quality. Green wood can also cause creosote to build up on the inside of your chimney, which is one of the leading causes of chimney fires.

So, whether you are using an open fire or a wood burner, all firewood should be seasoned properly before you burn it (see Seasoning, page 104). Green wood will sizzle, hiss or even bubble on the fire and produce lots of smouldering smoke, rather than a hot, clean flame. You can also tell if wood is green from its weight – wet wood is heavier than the equivalent seasoned log.

On a camping trip, if you don't have any alternative, there are a few tree species that you can burn green. The same issues remain – namely that most of the fire's energy will be used to evaporate the water rather than heating you up – but ash, birch, holly and sycamore will all burn green.

Seasoning

Seasoned wood burns hotter, cleaner and greener than wet wood. But different trees take different lengths of time to dry out. Different thicknesses of wood also season at different rates. So how do you know when your logs are ready to burn? Not all of the following apply to every species, so use a combination of checks to be sure:

- *Cracks* – look for radial cracks and splits on the log, the more the better.

- *Colour* – seasoned wood loses its vibrant colour. Choose faded, pale and grey logs.

- *Chips* – bark should fall off easily; the drier the wood, the looser the bark.

- *Splinters* – dry wood will be prone to splintering.

- *Smell* – wet wood smells strongly of sap; dry wood has a delicate woody aroma.

- *Sound* – knock two pieces together. You want a hollow clunk rather than a dull thud.

For accuracy, use a moisture meter – these devices can give you an indication of the percentage of water in your firewood (see Moisture Meters, page 106) and work best if you test a sample of logs from any one load. Aim for 20%, and don't burn anything higher than 25%.

Different species take different times to season: dense hardwoods like oak, beech and hornbeam may take two years to fully season, while conifers and fast-growing broadleaves like ash and birch can be ready in a year (see the Tree Table for suggested seasoning times, page 72).

Whichever variety you choose, you can speed up the drying process in three ways – more heat, greater airflow and smaller log size. Keep narrower logs in a warm, dry, well-ventilated store (like a boiler shed) and your firewood seasoning times drop dramatically.

Moisture Meters

If you want to test how dry your logs are, invest in a moisture meter. These simple, hand-held devices tell you in seconds whether the firewood you've just had delivered is seasoned, or can give you an accurate idea of how much further your log stack has to dry.

Most moisture meters have two sharp prongs on the end, which you press into the piece of timber you're testing. The meter uses a low electrical current to test the proportion of water to wood in any given sample. Sounds easy, but logs have a habit of giving off unreliable readings, especially if you test the outside of a crateful or the dry end of damp log.

The wettest part of any log will be at its heart, so you'll need to *split any wood you are testing*. Just prodding the end or pre-split surface (which dries out more quickly) will give you a false reading. Equally, if you have a well-seasoned crate of logs that's just been rained on, testing the outer surfaces would give too wet a reading.

As with any good experiment, *test more than one log*. A mix of samples, from inside and outside the stack or crate will help even out any huge variations. You should also *test in more than one spot on the same log* and average the results. Remember – you want a reading of around 20% or less, and certainly no more than 25%.

Double-Drying

Timber is like a sponge. It can both absorb and release water, depending on how much moisture is in the air around it. In most outdoor conditions, seasoned firewood will never be drier than around 12-18% moisture content.

But indoor air is often drier than this. Thanks to central heating, better insulation and plenty of roaring fires, during the winter months the air in the average home contains much less moisture than outside (which is why some of us get dry skin). We can use this to our advantage and bring seasoned wood indoors for a last blast of extra drying.

Which poses the question – why don't you dry all green wood indoors? In theory you could, but you'd need plenty of air movement, heat and space. It's just not practical for most of us. Also, the moisture from the green timber has to go somewhere – you don't want that amount of extra moisture indoors, where it can cause damp, mould and other issues.

Stick to seasoned wood, and view double-drying as a top-up. Simply bring in your seasoned wood and store it near your heat source (but not too near – see Staying Safe – Indoors, page 150) or radiator, in a container that allows air movement (a large wicker basket is ideal). Even if it's just for a few days, it all helps.

N.B. Some wood-burning stoves have metal log stores underneath, but don't be tempted to stack logs against the sides of the stove – it's a serious fire risk.

Log Baskets

You need to get your fuel from the log store to the fireside. And you also need somewhere to store timber by the fireside. There are lots of different options out there, from log holders to baskets, iron frames to log bags – ultimately it's down to practicality and preference.

One of the problems is that anything big enough to take a decent amount of logs is often too heavy to carry. If you use the same basket to

transport logs and to keep them by the fire, you also tend to leave an annoying trail of bark and debris in your wake. From experience, the best solution is to have a combination of static baskets and portable log carriers. That way, you can dash out to the log store and grab a manageable amount of timber in one go, without having to disrupt your fireside arrangement.

Kindling Bucket – Have a small bucket or basket by the fireside, primed with small, dry pieces. Even better if it has a handle so you can fill it up outside and bring it in.

Log Basket – Choose a large, sturdy basket or wooden crate that's robust enough to take logs being dumped into it from a height. If you've got room for two baskets, even better; that way you can double dry.

Log Carrier – Fetching logs in by the armful is fine, but it might damage your clothes. Canvas log bags will carry a sizeable load and fold away when you don't need them. Look for strong handles and wipeable fabric.

CHAPTER FIVE

Starting a Fire

'Education is not the filling of a pail,
but the lighting of a fire.'

W.B. YEATS

The Young Fire

The first five or ten minutes of a fire are the most crucial and, potentially, the most frustrating. It's a process that can't be rushed, involving a sequence that allows the fire to grow in stages. The next chapter gives you lots of different ways to construct the perfect fire, but here are a few things to check before you even light the paper...

Open the air supply. Whether it's opening the damper or pulling out the air vent on a wood burner, don't forget your fire needs plenty of oxygen.

Have your tinder or firelighters ready. Make sure you've already got plenty of newspaper scrumpled into balls, your tinder heaped in a mound, or your firelighters ready.

Don't scrimp on kindling. Use handfuls of very dry, thin kindling at this stage, and make sure there's space between the kindling to let air circulate.

Be patient. Don't try to do everything at once (unless you're making a Top-Down Fire) – put too much timber, or logs that are too wide, on the fire to begin with and it can smother the flames.

Maintain the heat. Develop a sense for how your fire is coping. If the fire looks as though it's struggling, add smaller logs to raise the temperature. If it's burning too fast and flames are roaring up the chimney, add a larger log to bring the heat down. The aim is to have plenty of glowing heat without too many flames. You'll soon get a feel for it.

Firelighters

Traditionally, you start a fire with tinder and a flame. The flame ignites the tinder, the tinder ignites the kindling, the kindling ignites the logs. Finding suitable, dry tinder isn't always easy, so firelighters are a reliable, quick alternative and cut out one stage of the fire-building process if you're in a hurry.

The downside is that most commercial firelighter cubes contain a number of either polluting or toxic ingredients, such as kerosene or urea-formaldehyde. They are also poisonous if ingested – not ideal if you have small children or pets around. Always keep firelighters out of reach of little hands and paws.

Thankfully, there's an increasing movement towards eco-friendly firelighters, made from a whole host of flammable, non-toxic ingredients such as vegetable oils, beeswax, wood shavings, sawdust and woodchip. Not only are they less polluting, but they also tend to be odour free, which makes them useful if you are lighting a cooking fire (see Fire and Cooking , page 33).

Liquid firelighters are only designed for outdoor use, such as bonfires and campfires, and are NOT suitable for indoor fires and wood burners. Not only do they release vapours that are toxic if inhaled, they are also potentially explosive. You should also never use liquid firelighters to 'refresh' a fire – whether indoor or outdoor – as the fumes can ignite and cause severe burns. Only use liquid firelighter on an unlit fire, allowing the liquid to soak into the kindling before lighting it with a long safety match. The safest brands of liquid firelighter have child-resistant caps and anti-flashback nozzles.

N.B. NEVER use an accelerant to light a fire. Petrol and liquid paraffin both give off powerful vapours. When you pour an accelerant onto a fire, the flames can follow the vapours back and up to the source, i.e. you or the petrol can in your hand.

Homemade Firelighters

If you want to make your own firelighters, this is an easy recipe. You can use traditional candle wax, but both soy wax and beeswax are non-petroleum-based, making them better for the environment and indoor air quality. The addition of a few drops of essential oil means you can add spicy, wintery notes such as sandalwood, cinnamon and nutmeg. Homemade firelighters also make really pretty gifts.

- Pack of tealights (soy or beeswax if possible)

- Dry pine cones

- Tweezers

- A few drops of your favourite essential oils

- Paper cupcake cases

- Cupcake tin

1. Line the cupcake tin with the paper cases.

2. Remove the tealights from their metal tins and place one in each case.

3. In a moderate oven, melt the wax until it is liquid and the wick is floating.

4. Take out of the oven and add a few drops of essential oil to each mould. *

5. With tweezers, move the wick to the edge of paper case and sit a pine cone upright in the melted wax. Make sure the wick is still accessible.

6. When completely cool, peel away the paper case.

    *You could also add spices or herbal sprigs to the melted wax – try pine needles, lavender, rosemary or orange peel.

Tinder

Tinder is the foundation of a fire. If you don't have firelighters, or prefer to practise firecraft in its purest form, tinder is the material that will provide the first fuel for your fire and ignite any kindling. In survival situations, tinder needs to be combustible enough to catch with just the smallest of sparks, but for everyday fires, as long as it's dry and easily lit with a match, you're in business.

So what can you use as tinder? There are a surprising number of household and natural plant materials that work, but they always have three things in common – they have to be very dry, light and airy (if something is fluffy, it has a large surface area, which makes it easier to ignite).

In the home, tinder needs to be sustainable and cost-efficient, so scrunched-up newspaper is usually the first choice (glossy magazines and gift wrap don't burn well and can release noxious fumes). Wood shavings, cardboard loo rolls, brown paper bags, strands of dry plant material and pine cones also make excellent starter fuel. If you want to add a fragrant note to the fire, dried orange peel makes a pleasing and crackly fire starter, while birch bark and dry rosemary will also work well.

In a survival situation, or if you have no other means of lighting an indoor fire, you can resort to lint (from your pocket or tumble dryer), steel wool, potato crisps, candle stubs, cigarette filters, dry moss, tampons, cotton wool balls, string, dry grasses/pine needles/leaves, and plants with fluffy seed heads (such as milkweed, bulrushes, catkins, dandelion clocks).

Kindling

Once you've got your tinder or firelighters lit, it's the kindling's turn to do its work. It needs to burn long enough to set fire to the first few logs, so make sure it's dry, thinly split and stacked with plenty of air space in between.

Some things make better kindling than others. Softwood comes into its own here – the sap-rich timber makes it ideal for easy lighting and fast burning – and if you can get hold of 'fatwood', the resin-impregnated heartwood of coniferous trees, even better. Cedar wood also makes cracking kindling.

If you are splitting your own kindling, aim for as small as you dare – invariably you'll get a mix of sizes, but if you're averaging sticks of about 2 centimetres (¾ in) by 2 centimetres, that's perfect. Make as much kindling in one go as you can, and don't scrimp on it when you're laying the fire – it can take a surprising amount of heat to ignite the first thick logs. Keep a generous metal bucketful near the fire; the rest can be stored outside, bagged up or kept in bins until it's needed.

You can also supplement your kindling with other shreds of natural material. Dry bark, birch or sycamore twigs, lumber scraps, dry corncobs and large pine cones will all help your fire burn.

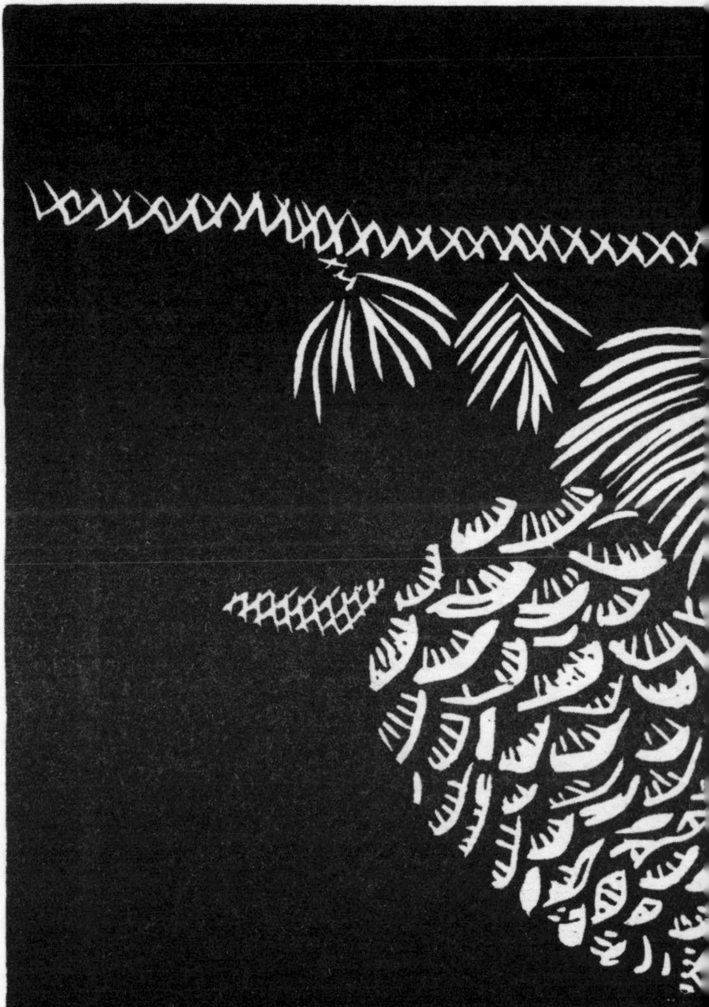

Matches and Lighters

Does it really matter what you light your fire with? Well, probably not. But in terms of convenience and chances of not getting singed, some products are better than others:

Extra-Long Matches – A normal, short match gives you about six seconds before it reaches your fingers. For most open fires and campfires, this just isn't enough time to light the tinder or newspaper, especially if you want it to catch in more than one place. Extra-long matches are brilliant for two reasons – not only do they give you more time to light the fire, often three or four times longer, but they also allow you to place the flame right inside the heart of your kindling and tinder. They're also called hearth matches or long-reach matches.

Barbeque Gas Lighters – If you've got children and don't want matches hanging around, long-necked gas lighters are a good alternative. They also allow a long reach into the fire and will keep a flame alive for more than enough time to get things started. Look for lighters that have child-safety locks and are refillable.

Waterproof Matches – Sometimes called stormproof matches, these ingenious igniters have an extra-large head and will light (and stay lit) even in heavy wind or rain. They don't give you a long burn – usually only about ten seconds – so you wouldn't want them for everyday hearth use, but are an absolute lifesaver on a camping trip or survival expedition.

How to Strike a Match

It might seem obvious how to strike a match, but if you're down to your last few and they keep snapping or going out, it's important to know you're doing it right.

1. Kneel next to the fire. You don't want the match to have to travel any distance to the tinder.

2. Hold your match between your thumb and index finger.

3. Support the head of the match with your middle finger – this reduces the chance of the head snapping off.

4. Turn your hand so your palm is facing downwards.

5. Push the match forwards along the strikeplate, i.e. away from you, not towards you. This is for two reasons: one, if the lit head snaps off you have a fighting chance of it landing on the kindling, and two, it

prevents sparks being directed towards your clothing.

And if you're lighting a campfire, you need to think about how the weather will affect the match:

6. Protect the flame. Use your hands and body to shield the lit match from any gusts or driving rain.

7. Light the base of the fire. The first precious flames will travel upwards through the fuel and have less chance of being blown out or extinguished by rain.

8. Face downwind. You want the wind to be behind you. This does two things: your body is shielding the campfire from any driving weather, and you're reducing the chance of flames leaping back in your direction.

Scrunching Newspaper

Do we need to scrunch newspaper to light a fire? Talk to ten different real-fire enthusiasts and you'll get ten different answers. Some prefer the rolled newspaper technique, others shred, but most people stick to scrunching up newspaper into tight balls.

If you look at the science, there's actually sound logic behind it. When you scrunch up a large piece of paper into spheres, it does three things, all of which help you if you are lighting a fire. The first is that it increases the surface area of the paper relative to the size of the ball. A grapefruit-sized ball of newspaper is relatively small, but thanks to its many folds and creases, it has a huge surface area. Put a handful of these paper balls into a fireplace, and you have crammed a generous amount of potential fuel into a fairly restricted space.

The second reason is that scrunched-up paper is incredibly strong and can bear a substantial weight on top of it – perfect for stacking kindling and logs on top. Try doing the same with shredded newspaper; it just doesn't work. And last, but equally importantly, even when you scrunch newspaper into the smallest ball you can manage, it's still 90% air. Air plus fuel equals the perfect recipe for combustion.

CHAPTER SIX

Building a Fire

'He sat in the snow, pulling the sticks from the bushes under the trees and feeding them directly to the flame. He knew he must not fail. When it is 75 below zero, a man must not fail in his first attempt to build a fire.'

JACK LONDON, *To Build a Fire*

Which Fire to Build?

This is the fun bit. There are dozens of different ways to construct a fire, each with an army of faithful supporters. Until recently, most people relied on the traditional bottom-up fire, with newspaper and kindling at the base and logs on the top. In recent years, many wood-fire enthusiasts have been extolling the virtues of the Top-Down fire, the counterintuitive method of upside-down burning (see The Top-Down Fire, page 141).

The reality is that every fire, fireplace and wood stove is different. Timber supplies vary, as do airflow and access to good kindling. This makes it difficult to generalize – what works for one home may not for another. The trick is to experiment. Work out which method suits the size and idiosyncrasies of your hearth or log burner.

If you're outdoors, the weather conditions may influence what kind of fire you build – the Lean-To Fire, for example, is a good one to build if you need to protect the fledgling flames from wind or driving rain. If you want to cook on your fire with some degree of control, the Cowboy Fire works a treat.

Whichever method you choose, if you are outdoors you can also boost any heat the fire kicks out by building a simple reflector. Push two thin poles into the ground, leaning slightly away from the fire. Stack logs horizontally up the sticks to create a barrier, or lean anything reflective against them, and this will throw back some of that lost heat.

The Bottom-Up Fire

Whether you build a teepee of sticks or the more complex log-cabin, this type of fire essentially burns from the bottom up. The logic of this is that flames flicker upwards and ignite the fuel above. In practice, radiant heat travels in multiple directions (which is why the Top-Down Fire also works), but this method has the advantage of keeping your newspaper or tinder dry if there's any rain. You can also build a smaller, quicker fire this way, keeping it to just a few sticks. With all bottom-up fires, leave putting the largest logs on until you are confident the fire has taken hold.

The Teepee – start with the tinder or firelighter in the middle, and lean the kindling sticks over it, tips pointing upwards, to create a wigwam shape. If

the stack is stable enough, you can build up the sides with progressively larger logs.

Suitable for: open fires, wood burners and campfires. Simple, easy and doesn't need much initial fuel – perfect for a small fire.

The Log-Cabin – take two kindling sticks and place them parallel to each other, about 10 centimetres (4 in) apart. Take two more sticks and balance them across the first two, creating four sides of a square. Continue stacking pairs of kindling until you are about six layers high. Fill the middle with tinder and then make a 'roof' from a layer of kindling topped with thin logs.

Suitable for: open fires and campfires. A bit too fiddly for a wood burner. Takes longer to build but low maintenance and slow burning once lit.

The Sandwich – a traditional hearth fire. Start with a layer of crumpled newspaper or firelighters. Add three layers of kindling (criss-cross the layers and leave plenty of air gaps), followed by two or three narrow logs.

Suitable for: open fires and wood burners. Quick to build and lights relatively easily. Not ideal for campfires as struggles to catch if windy.

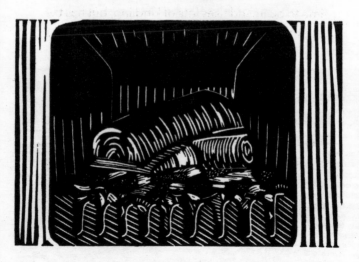

The Top-Down Fire

If you haven't tried this method, do. Even if it's just to prove that it works. It feels completely counterintuitive, after years of fire-building bottom-up, but more often than not it produces results. It's also a handy technique for wood-burning stoves, which often have a log guard or grill at the front that can make accessing the base of a fire tricky.

Suitable for: large open fires, wood burners and campfires (only in good weather). Takes some time to build and uses lots of kindling, but has the advantage of pre-warming the flue, helping it draw.

Where top-down fires don't perform as well tends to be if the logs or tinder aren't dry enough, there isn't enough room in the wood burner to create a decent stack, or if you're outdoors and there's a chance your tinder will be blown away or rained on before it's had chance to catch. It's also a fire stack that needs a generous amount of kindling to work, so if you're in short supply, stick to the Teepee.

Indoors, the top-down method has the advantage of pre-warming the flue, which helps draw the smoke up the chimney, and it also allows you to make a relatively large fire in one go, letting you get on with other things. The trick with this fire is to take your time while you are building it – the more stable the structure, the less likely it is to collapse and potentially go out.

1. Lay your largest logs in a row on the hearth, ground or in the base of your wood burner. Leave a 2.5 centimetre (1 in) gap between them to allow for air movement.

2. Take your narrow logs and lay them on top, perpendicular to the first row.

3. Continue with two or three layers of kindling, again perpendicular to each other, and top with a final layer of tinder or newspaper. Secure the tinder or paper with a few extra sticks of kindling on top.

The Lean-To Fire

This is a good one if you are out in the sticks and struggling against the elements, as the inherent design of the fire acts as a windbreak to protect the first flames. It's also a very stable structure.

1. Find a thick, dry log and use this as your 'brace log'. You could also use a large stone.

2. Lean small twigs or any other kindling against the brace log, making sure they are on the downwind side (i.e. the brace log is shielding the twigs from the wind.) You can make this fire as short or long as you wish, depending on how far along the log you prop your kindling.

3. Fill underneath the kindling with dry tinder.

   Once the fire is established, keep adding fuel to the downwind side of the log, but don't prop it against the brace log. The

brace log will char and burn very slowly, acting more as a windbreak than the focus of the fire. In fact, once the embers are glowing, you can add another brace log on the other side of the fire, parallel to the first, and you have yourself a makeshift cooking platform.

Suitable for: campfires, even if the weather's bad. Can be turned into a cooking fire. Will work as an indoor fire, but the brace log can take up too much space in a small hearth or wood burner.

The Cowboy Fire

This name conjures up images of Wild West cowboys eating beans out of mess tins. In reality, this fire, also called the Star Fire, isn't particularly practical to sit around as the radiating 'spokes' of the fire are a bit of a trip hazard and keep you at a distance from the heat.

What it does make is a cracking cooking fire. This is because all the heat is focused into one small, intense spot – ideal for straddling with a metal tripod and hanging cooking pot. Because the ends of the logs are also near each other, they make the perfect platform for resting a metal grill or griddle pan on.

It's also a brilliant one for outdoors if you have no means of cutting long lengths of timber down – as the fire nibbles away the ends of the logs, you simply push them further into the centre.

1. Lay between six and ten long logs in a star shape (like the spokes of a wheel).

2. Where the spokes meet in the middle, leave a gap the size of a side plate and

fill with tinder. On top of this, layer plenty of kindling. The kindling should be long enough to stretch across the gap and sit on the ends of the logs. This helps with airflow.

3. Keep adding tinder and small pieces of fuel until the ends of the logs start to burn. Once the fire is well established, remember to keep nudging the logs into the heat.

Suitable for: campfires and large open fires. Too big for a wood burner – the large footprint needs a generous hearth space. Great for cooking, uses little wood and slow burning.

Fireside Tools

Every fireside needs a companion set. These aren't just quaint decorative items, but tools you'll use every time you build, burn and clean up after a fire. Here's what the set should contain:

Poker – for manoeuvring burning materials around the fireplace and, when the fire's over, spreading out the hot embers. Coal benefits from regular prodding, but don't be tempted to overdo it with a wood fire; all you'll get is a shower of sparks. Get a poker with a hook so you can pull logs as well as push them.

Tongs – should the occasional piece of burning material escape or get out of place, tongs are essential. Don't get coal tongs, which are essentially like a large pair of tweezers; you need log tongs, which have a scissor action that can grab large pieces of wood.

Brush and Metal Shovel – needed for ash removal and removing debris brought in with the log basket. The brush needs to have robust natural bristles (e.g. coir) that won't melt on contact with heat.

Heatproof Gloves – handy if you have a wood-burning stove with a metal door handle or air vent that gets hot during operation. They can also double up as protection from splintery logs and kindling.

Bellows – these give a struggling fire the extra boost of air it needs to take hold. To use bellows, aim the nozzle at pieces of glowing timber, and blow only until they start to flame. On a new fire, go gently; you don't want to blow out the first flames.

Staying Safe – Indoors

Whether you're having an open fire or using a log burner, unfortunately the home is where most accidents are likely to happen. Anyone who uses a fire, or lives in a home heated by wood, should be aware of the potential hazards so you can take steps to prevent accidents and keep everyone safe:

- Keep flues clean and well maintained – this reduces the chance of a chimney fire.

- Have your chimney swept at least twice a year if you are burning logs – at the beginning and in the middle of the season.

- Make sure there is plenty of ventilation.

- Always get wood-burning stoves and flues fitted by a qualified professional.

- Use a robust meshed guard to protect against flying sparks.

- Keep children away from open fires and wood burners – use a safety guard with fixed wall brackets.

- Don't go to bed until you are sure that the fire is under control and guarded or, ideally, completely out.

- Don't prop logs against wood burners, where they can heat up and smoulder.

- Don't dry clothes over or near the fire.

- Keep matches, lighters and firelighters out of reach of children and pets.

- Don't burn wet wood, plastics, rubbish or any other materials likely to give off smoke, noxious fumes and particulates.

- Get smoke and carbon monoxide alarms if you haven't already.

Staying Safe – Outdoors

We often get complacent around campfires, but there's a huge responsibility attached to building a fire outdoors. Forest fires are a common occurrence in many parts of the world, and all too often started by an unwitting camper, but closer to home you've still got to be vigilant around farmland, dry crops and even your neighbour's prized picket fence.

- Always check the weather forecast first. Sudden gusts of wind or changes of direction can soon whip up a campfire into a wildfire.

- Choose a safe spot to build your fire. Build on level ground covered with gravel or soil if possible, and steer well clear of overhanging branches, tents, vehicles, fences, dry grass – stay 3 metres (10 ft) from anything that could catch.

- Don't use accelerants to light or revive a fire and, after lighting it, don't throw the match away until you've doused it with water.

- Keep your supply of dry firewood upwind, away from any flying sparks and hot ashes.

- Kids need to be supervised at all times. Teach them how to stop, drop and roll if their clothing catches fire.

- Never leave your campfire unattended, and keep a bucket of water handy at all times.

- When it's time to go, extinguish the fire by drowning it with water and stirring the embers to make sure everything is cold. Don't bury the embers with soil; they can smoulder.

Ashes

This fine, soft, light-grey powder is manna from heaven for gardeners as it's full of lime, potassium and other trace elements that plants need to flourish. Traditionally, wood ash was also used as an abrasive cleaning agent and as an ingredient in soap making, and it still has plenty of uses today:

Fertilizer – Sprinkle lightly over the beds and lawn or rake into soil. You can also tip it straight into your compost heap, where it'll mellow and add to the richness of the organic matter.

Soil improver – Add to very acidic soil (5.5 pH or less) to raise the pH level – tomatoes and other nightshade vegetables love it. Don't use on raspberries, however, which like slightly acidic soil, as do roses and rhododendrons.

Pest repellent – Wood ash makes life very uncomfortable for snails and slugs; place a ring around the most affected plants. Ash has also been known to be effective against aphids when dusted onto tomato plants and aubergines.

Household cleaner – Mix with a little water to form a smooth paste, apply it to silverware and then let it sit for a few minutes. Wipe off and buff to a shine.

De-icer – Wood ash also makes a good eco-friendly de-icer, perfect for throwing over pavements and driveways. The ash works mainly by increasing traction, but the salts in ash also have a gentle de-icing effect.

N.B. Ashes can stay hot for a long time after the fire has died out. Always store them away from combustible material, in a metal container or bucket.

CHAPTER SEVEN

The Fragrant Fire

'Old wood best to burn,
old wine to drink,
old friends to trust,
and old authors to read.'

ALFONSO X OF CASTILE

Scented Smoke

In most instances, you don't want a smoky fire. If your hearth is billowing out grey swirling clouds, you're either burning wet wood, there's not enough oxygen getting to the wood, or your chimney's blocked. But there are occasions where smoke is useful, even desirable. If you want to smoke meat or cheese, keep flying insects at bay, or add a whiff of woody scent to a room, a little smoke can go a long way.

There are different ways to get your fire to produce smoke, as you'll see in the following pages, but you are, in essence, deliberately creating a situation where the fire can't combust completely. When woodfuel can't combust completely, not everything is burned away, and what you can see are tiny unburned particles of things like tar, carbon (soot), oils and ash floating upwards with the fire's warm convected air.

But is it healthy to breathe in woodsmoke? There's no doubt that persistent exposure to lungfuls of sooty smoke is not only irritating but potentially harmful in the long term. But that isn't what we're aiming for – we're talking about scented smoke wafting through the air to draw you close to the fire, spices and herbs crackling in the open flames, and gently smouldering applewood chips. Think of the fragrant fire as a huge incense stick – an ancient device to give out warming, aromatic wisps of delicious smoke. It's interesting to note that the word 'perfume' comes from the Latin *perfumare*, meaning 'to smoke through', and a time when smoke was used not only for room fragrance but for religious rituals and purification.

Perfumed Wood

Not all wood smells delicious when it burns, but there's a generous basketful of species that will add wisps of pleasant, aromatic smoke to an open fire. Most of the smoke will appear at the beginning of your evening, when the fire isn't hot enough to combust completely, so make the most of this time to add your fragrant kindling and logs. Once the fire is well established you can, if you're careful, use a poker to separate a log from the others and allow it to smoulder gently without flames for a few minutes before pushing it back into the heart of the fire.

So which wood smells good? Much is down to personal preference – one man's perfume is another man's pollutant – but most people find that fruit trees such as apple, cherry, pear, fig and plum give off a gentle, subtly sweet scent. Soft coniferous woods, such as pine and spruce, produce a pleasant, resinous smoke, while nut species like hazel and walnut add oaty, autumnal notes.

Some of the hardwoods – oak, elm, ash and birch – have homely, campfire smells, but the stars of the show have to be cedar, hickory and mesquite, three woods that you don't often see sold as firewood but have the most fantastically evocative smoke (and are sold as chips – see Smoking Food, page 176). Other richly scented woods that don't often get logged but may come your way in the form of garden cuttings and branches include eucalyptus, olive, bay and cypress.

Pine Cones

There are few things more Christmassy than the smell of spruce. Pine cones – those woody, tactile pockets of scent – are the perfect way to capture that feeling, and make excellent kindling for an aromatic fire.

Despite their seasonal connotations, pine cones actually drop throughout most of the year, depending on the species of tree, weather conditions, and whether the cone is male or female. Autumn is probably the most fruitful time to go a-hunting, so gather and keep as many basketfuls as you dare, to dry out and store by the fire.

The pine cone makes a particularly good fire starter for two reasons: first, those thin wood scales are perfect for catching light and help the cone dry out to a useful moisture level, and second, their glorious sticky resin is highly flammable. As with all pine material, burning pine cones can leave a small amount of creosote deposits on the inside of the chimney, but with the volumes you'll burn the impact will be minimal and negated by a twice-yearly sweep.

For maximum combustion, make sure the pine cones are lovely and dry, with the prickles as open as possible. Some people actually dry theirs in a low oven first – a thirty-minute blast is ample – and then add a few drops of pine essential oil to each cone for extra fragrance. Use a handful at a time.

Herb Bundles

The idea of herb bundles (also called smudge sticks and herb cakes) isn't a new one. For thousands of years, people have used aromatic smoke to bless, cleanse and heal – ceremonies and sacred spaces were filled with the scents of burning herbs, resin and bark. In medieval times, herbs were dried and tied ready to toss onto an open fire to sweeten the air and stave off ill-health.

The best time to make herb bundles is after the summer flourish has died down, when you're pruning back those woody aromatic herbs. Start well before the first frosts – not only will this give the plants time to recover, but you'll also have created a nice dry basketful of herb bundles ready for the log-fire season.

You need cuttings or prunings of about 15 centimetres (6 in). Choose any fragrant herbs – the woodier the better, as they'll survive the drying process intact. Rosemary, bay, lavender, eucalyptus, thyme, lemon verbena, sage – there's a whole apothecary of herbs to try. Tie a handful together with natural string or raffia, and experiment with combinations of herbs for different aromas.

These fragrant bundles will not only gently perfume the living room while stacked patiently in a basket, but throw a few on the fire, either at the very beginning or on the embers at the very end, and you'll be rewarded with a gentle waft of incense-like smoke.

Peel and Spices

Citrus peel and spices add a heady mulled-wine note to the fragrant fire. As the components are smaller and fiddlier, you need to wrap them in newspaper; making Christmas-cracker-like twists works a treat, and the shape makes them easier to light at one end.

Whole spices are expensive, so this is a good way to recycle aromatics that have already had one round in a recipe. Vanilla pods scraped of their seeds still have lots of sweet-smelling potential, as do cinnamon pods that have been simmered, cloves from a ham, or bay leaves fished out of a stock pot. Just dry them off and add to the mix.

Similarly, bought citrus peel is too expensive to burn, but you can easily dry your own anywhere that's warm and airy. Lay on a plate and rest it on the Aga, at the back of the airing cupboard or propped on a radiator, and the peel will be dry in days. Tangerine, satsuma, orange, lemon and clementine peels are brilliant oily fire starters and really give these bundles some oomph.

To make the bundles:

1. Take a double-spread sheet of broadsheet newspaper and fold along the crease. Use black-and-white pages only (coloured ink or glossy pages can release noxious fumes).

2. At one end of the sheet, place a handful of dried citrus peel and whole spices – cloves, cinnamon sticks, star anise, cardamom pods, cumin, coriander seeds, used vanilla pods, spent coffee grounds, fennel seeds – create your own blend, but always include plenty of peel as that's the tinder that will really catch.

3. Roll up the newspaper and twist both ends to make a cracker shape – this will stop the spices falling out. Use in place of other tinder.

Fragrant Firelighters

Traditional firelighters do the job but contribute very little to the fragrant fire. At best, they're odourless; at worst, they can leave a pungent whiff of burning fossil fuels and give an unpleasant tinge to food if you're cooking on an outdoor fire.

If you want the convenience but don't want to sacrifice scent, there are an increasing number of natural firelighters on the market, ready to light, and studded with delicious-smelling herbs, spices and peel.

Some are candle-wax based, usually soy or beeswax, as that gives a less polluting burn. They are often perfumed with essential oils – orange or cinnamon, for example – and then topped with woody notes such as cinnamon shavings and star anise.

Pine cones set into wax are another eco-option (see Homemade Firelighters, page 118 for a DIY version). The wax is a good vehicle for other flammable ingredients such as pine needles and wood shavings. You can even get them set into old egg cartons, so you can just tear off a segment and throw it into the fire.

A less well-known option are ocote firesticks. Ocote is a fast-growing timber from Central America traditionally used by the Mayan people for lighting fires. The species is a member of the coniferous family and has a naturally high resin content that catches quickly, making it ideal fodder for firelighting. Ocote also has the good fortune to be highly fragrant, and once lit, produces an intense and deliciously piney perfume – perfect for fans of scented smoke.

Essential Oils

It's worth prefacing anything about perfumes and fragrant fires with the gentle warning that essential oils are highly flammable, so it's not ideal to start throwing them onto hot embers or naked flames. Don't even keep the bottle near the fire.

But their very flammability, combined with their potent fragrance, makes them eminently useful when added as an ingredient to wax firelighters, or if a few drops of heady scent are left to soak into and dry onto pine cones or other tinder and kindling. This has the added benefit of turning your pine-cone basket into a huge pot-pourri, exuding welcoming smells even when the fire's out.

Certain scents work better than others – the smell of burning rose oil, the epitome of a summer's day, for example, can feel incongruous on a cosy winter's evening, so head for essential oils that capture those resinous, evocative aromas of log piles and herb bundles (see Herb Bundles, page 166), or conjure up wintery celebrations and memories:

- *Sandalwood* – sweet, warm, rich, masculine and woody

- *Cypress* – clean, fresh, herbaceous, slightly evergreen

- *Cedarwood* – soft, woody, not unlike pencil sharpenings

- *Frankincense* – sweetly spicy, honeyed, slightly fruity

- *Myrhh* – smoky, sweet, earthy, some say liquorice-like

- *Pine* – fresh, foresty, like Christmas in a bottle

- *Cinnamon* – warm, homely, spicy – the smell of hot cross buns

- *Eucalyptus* – strong, camphor-like, reminiscent of chesty cough rub.

Smoking Food

Fragrant smoke triggers all kinds of primeval responses. Just as we feel comforted and protected by the smell of an open fire, so too are our taste buds sharpened by a whiff of woody smoke. As humans, we associate the smell of fire not only with heat and security, but also with the anticipation of cooked food – our inner caveman doesn't sit far below the surface.

The process is subtle, and you can tweak the results depending on the type of woodchips or shavings you burn. Woodsmoke varies in flavour from mild to strong; delicate foods that you don't want to overpower – salmon, vegetables, cheeses and chicken – need a light touch, while gutsier meats – beef, lamb, game and pork – are transformed with strongly flavoured woods:

- *Apple* – a gentle, fruity smoke flavour that works with poultry, fish and pork. All the fruit woods are mild flavoured and ideal for smoking cheeses, butter and vegetables.

- *Oak* – a mellow, well-rounded smoky flavour, delicious with almost every foodstuff. You can also buy oak chips from whisky barrels, which gives an extra dimension to the flavour.

- *Maple* – another mellow-flavoured smoke that adds a sweet, subtle flavour perfect for poultry, game birds, ham and cheeses.

- *Hickory* – the quintessentially American flavour of smoked bacon. Strongly flavoured so works best with pork, ribs and other barbeque favourites.

- *Mesquite* – very strongly flavoured, but slightly sweeter than hickory, and paired best with rich, red meats such as steak, duck or lamb.

Smoke and Allergies

Not everyone finds smoke pleasant. While most of us thrill at the sight of a roaring fire, there are some people who find smoke difficult to tolerate, particularly those with any kind of respiratory problem.

If you suffer from allergic rhinitis or asthma, is there anything you can do to alleviate the problem while still enjoying the conviviality of a real fire? The first thing to say is that open fires, for all their contemplative cosiness, throw far more smoke and irritating particles back into the room than a closed stove, so you may find that investing in a certified wood burner dramatically reduces any problems.

Air pollution is also worse if wood isn't seasoned properly, the chimney is clogged up or there isn't adequate airflow getting to the fuel. Keeping to sensible woodfuel practices, such as never burning wet wood, getting your chimney swept twice a year and making sure you know how to work the air vents on your wood-burning stove, is essential.

Some people find the mould on firewood can trigger problems, so if that's the case, don't store your logs indoors and only bring them in when you are ready to burn them. Other irritants might not come from the timber, but rather the other things that are being burned, such as petrochemical firelighters, rubbish, plastics or coloured paper. All these steps may help, but if you still find your symptoms are worsened by woodsmoke, you may need to reduce or eliminate your exposure altogether.

CHAPTER EIGHT

Fire Safety

'Man is the only creature that
dares to light a fire and live with it.
The reason? Because he alone has
learned to put it out.'

HENRY JACKSON VAN DYKE, JR,
Fisherman's Luck and Some Other Uncertain Things

The Yearly Check-Up

Your fireplace or stove is a tool, to be looked after, cleaned and repaired if necessary – do this and it will give you a long life of efficient, companionable warmth in return. When domestic fires go wrong, nine times out of ten it's down to poor maintenance, so here's a list of things you should check at least once a year, preferably well before the burning season gets going. Most people get their flues swept and buy fuel when the nights turn cool, but if you plan ahead you'll beat the rush and may even find things cheaper than in peak season.

Get your fuel supply – Don't get caught out and have to wait for logs to arrive. Buy early and get some extra seasoning time under your belt.

Call the sweep – Get the detritus from last winter's burn out of your flue before you spark up for the new season. If you are burning lots of wood, you may need an extra sweep mid burning season.

Service the stove – Check the condition of the key parts of your wood burner, such as the baffle plate, the rope seal around the door and the firebricks at the back. If you're not sure how to do this, ask a HETAS engineer.

Clean the glass – Even with good-quality fuel and a healthy airflow, your stove's door will have a tendency to blacken, especially at the corners. Use stove glass cleaner, and always wait until the wood burner is cool before you start.

Sweeps

Having your chimney swept is an absolute necessity. A chimney must be clear to allow noxious gases to pass up and out of your home instead of billowing back into your living room. Regular sweeping also removes all the sooty deposits that build up on the lining of the flue or brickwork, helping to prevent dangerous chimney fires.

While you can help reduce the likelihood of a blocked chimney by doing all the sensible things like not burning wet wood or banking up for overnight burning, the only sure-fire way to keep safe is to get it professionally swept. A qualified sweep will brush away the deposits from last season's fires, check the flue isn't blocked with nests or debris and keep an eye on the condition of key parts of your wood-burning stove or fireplace. Some insurance companies now insist on regular sweeping and will ask for paperwork to prove it.

If you want to find a reputable sweep, the best place to start is a regulatory trade organisation such as the Guild of Master Chimney Sweeps, National Association of Chimney Sweeps, Association of Professional Independent Chimney Sweeps, or HETAS (see Directory, page 202). To be a member of any of these bodies, candidates have to undergo training, be fully insured and work to a code of practice. And if you've never had your chimney swept before, don't be put off by visions of soot-covered brooms and clouds of dust – modern sweeps use strong vacuums, floor coverings and specialized tools to create minimal disruption and mess.

Fire and Furniture

A blazing fire is the beating heart of any room, the focal point around which everyone and everything should converge. It gives structure to a living space, a kinetic centrepiece that holds our attention and gives a room character and ambience. It's always good to position your furniture to capitalize on this cosiness, but how do you do it safely and with potentially flammable fabrics and upholstery in mind?

- Stick to the 1-metre rule – have nothing that is flammable, whether it's your sofa or your log basket, closer than 1 metre (3 ft) from the fire.

- Don't put mirrors above an open fireplace. People can end up standing too close to the flames and risk their clothes catching fire.

- Anything that is upholstered needs to meet current fire resistance standards – look for the label.

- Antiques and pre-1950s furniture are exempt from the standards, but it doesn't make them any less flammable. Keep these items further away from the fire.

- All fabrics can burn, but some are more resistant to catching than others. Pure wool, for example, is naturally slow to burn, while polyester-cotton blends can ignite and spread quickly.

- A hearth rug will not only soften the room but also protect a carpet or wooden floor from potential sparks. It must be flame resistant – look for those woven from flameproof fibreglass yarn, or natural fibres such as pure wool, jute or sisal, all of which are naturally fire retardant.

Smoke Control Areas

If you live in a town or city, there's a good chance your house is in a smoke control area. This means you can't let smoke roll out from your chimney unless you are burning an authorized fuel or using an exempt appliance. But what does that mean in practice?

Do I live in a smoke control area? If you're not sure, ring up your local council and ask the Environmental Services Department. They'll know.

If I do, does that mean I can't have an open fire? No. But it does mean you can only burn certain smokeless fuels on it, such as anthracite. Again, your local council will have a list of authorized fuels.

Is wood an authorized fuel? You can't burn normal logs, but you can burn heat logs, which are made from compressed waste wood and have fewer emissions (see Briquettes, page 85).

Can I have a wood-burning stove in a smoke control area? Yes, if it's an 'exempt appliance'. Most modern stoves are manufactured to burn very efficiently. The stove manufacturer will be able to tell you if it is on the exempt list. The list is also available from the Department for Environment, Food and Rural Affairs (see Directory, page 202).

If my wood burner is exempt, can I burn wood? Yes. But only use properly seasoned timber and stick to the manufacturer's recommendations.

What if my wood burner isn't exempt or I can't find out? The same rules apply as if it were an open fire, i.e. you can only burn authorized fuels.

And if I don't? The council can fine you up to £1000 in the UK.

Children

Children find fire mesmerizing. Exposure to risk and the life-enhancing skill of firecraft are important lessons, but only under the careful supervision of an adult. Fire is one of the most common causes of accidental injury and death amongst children, so it's vital that you teach them to respect and understand the dangers, as well as making your hearth and home as safe as possible.

Give clear, unambiguous instructions of dos and don'ts around fire. With young children under five, you will have to keep reinforcing the message. Key things to tell them include:

- Never to play with matches or lighters.

- If they see matches or lighters lying around, to tell a grown-up.

- Not to play or leave toys near an open fire or wood-burning stove.

As a responsible adult, the onus is on you to remove as many dangers as possible. It's all common sense but easy to overlook if you're busy or distracted:

- Don't leave young children on their own in a room where there's an open fire or lit wood burner.

- Keep matches, lighters and firelighters out of reach or locked away. Only use lighters with child-resistant features.

- Use a childproof fireguard in front of an open fire or wood burner (see Fireguards, page 192).

- Teach kids to stop, drop and roll – they'll love practising this, but it's a lifesaver if clothes accidentally catch fire.

- Make sure your children know what the smoke alarm sounds like, and practise, as a family, how you would escape and call 999.

Fireguards

There are two basic types of fireguard: the spark guard, which is a fine metal mesh designed to keep hot sparks from going astray, and the child-safety guard, a cage or fence-like guard with the sole purpose of keeping young kids at a safe distance from the source of heat.

Spark guards can be simple flat screens, which are useful if you have a large, recessed hearth and just need to cover the front of the fire. Most open fires, however, are safer with a hinged or folding guard, which can catch any stray sparks that ping off at a tangent.

Child-safety guards must create a physical barrier between the fire or hot stove and little fingers. Most manufacturers recommend a clear space of at least 75 centimetres (30 in) between the guard and the heat source. The guard also needs to be far enough away from direct heat so as not to become dangerously hot to touch. Child guards are designed to be fixed to the wall so a toddler can't fall and push the guard onto the flames or pull it on top of him or herself. These types of guards don't offer any spark protection, however, as the bars or grill meshes are too widely spaced, so if you've got an open fire and kids you'll need *both* types of guard.

Wood-burning stoves, while spark-safe, still need a child-safety guard – kids (and vulnerable adults) may not realize that even though the flame is safely contained, the metal is searingly hot to touch.

How to Check a Wood Burner

Wood burners are brilliantly simple, robust devices. There's not much that can go wrong with them, and when parts do wear out, they're relatively easy to fix. That said, if you've never owned one before, problems aren't always obvious without knowing what to look for. If you've inherited one with a house move, you *must* get the chimney swept and the stove looked over before you use it (see Sweeps, page 184). For the rest of the time, here are a few things to check on or watch for:

Firebricks – At the back and sides of the stove, firebricks protect the body of the wood burner from intense heat. If a brick is broken, replace it – a damaged brick can cause the stove to crack or distort.

Firerope – Fitted around the door, this flame-proof rope is designed to create a snug seal. Replace any missing or frayed rope and check the door closes tightly. Trap a piece of paper in the door – it should resist being pulled out.

Glass – A cracked glass screen needs replacing immediately, but it's an easy fix. Unscrew the tabs that keep it in place, measure up from the original glass and order replacement stove glass online or from a local glazier.

Rust – Exterior rust can conceal hidden problems. Remove with a wire brush and refinish with stove paint. Keep the interior rust-free by leaving the vent or door open during the summer months to encourage airflow.

Cracks or gaps – Look for cracks on the stove body or between the side and top plates. Never use a wood burner that could leak fumes – it'll need professional attention from a qualified engineer.

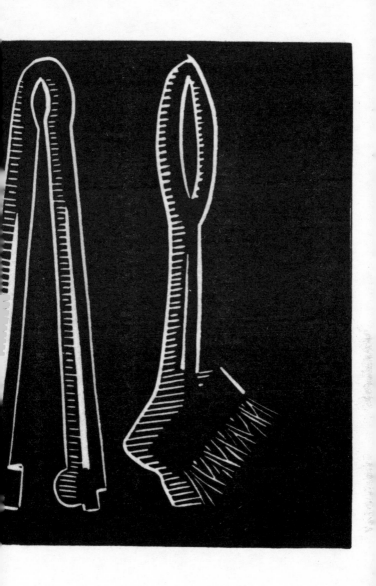

Carbon Monoxide and Smoke Alarms

Carbon monoxide is produced when fuels such as gas, coal and wood don't burn fully. Blocked chimneys, badly fitted wood burners and inadequate ventilation can all cause dangerous levels of CO to build up, with potentially fatal consequences. You can't smell, taste or see carbon monoxide, which is what makes it so deadly, but symptoms can include headaches, dizziness and loss of consciousness.

Along with getting your chimney swept regularly and having any stove installed by a qualified engineer, you MUST fit a carbon monoxide detector in any room with a fire. CO alarms are a legal requirement with stoves installed after 2010, and any stove in a rented property.

There are guidelines about where to fit your CO alarm. If you attach it to the ceiling, the alarm must be at least 30 centimetres (12 in) away from the wall. Alternatively it can be at head height, either on the wall or a shelf, approximately 1 to 3 metres (3 –10 ft) away from the fire. Make sure nothing is covering or obstructing the alarm, and don't fit it too close to a window, door or fan, or inside a cupboard.

Test the alarm once a week by pressing the 'test' or 'reset' button.

Along with a CO alarm, every home needs smoke alarms, especially if you are using open fires. Most fire services recommend at least one alarm on every floor, but ideally one alarm in every room you use regularly. Again, these need testing once a week.

Renting and Real Fires

With so many people renting, rather than buying, homes, it can be tricky to know how real fires fit into the scenario. Are you allowed to have an open fire or a wood burner? Whose responsibility is it to get the chimney swept? And who do you ask about smoke and CO alarms?

Landlord's responsibilities:

- To provide a smoke alarm on each storey and a carbon monoxide (CO) alarm in any room with a solid-fuel-burning appliance (i.e. an open fire or a wood-burning stove).

- To check the CO alarms and smoke alarms are in proper working order the day the tenancy commences.

- To check wood-burning stoves are serviced annually. Stoves installed after 2010 must have an installation certificate.

- To organize for the chimneys to be swept at the commencement of the tenancy and annually (or as specified in the property's insurance policy).

- To check and maintain any flues and ventilation.

- To repair any defective wood-burning stoves, fire hearths and surrounds, airbricks and ventilators.

Tenant's responsibilities:

- To regularly check the fire, smoke and CO alarms and replace the batteries when they run out.

- Never to leave live flames unattended (e.g. in open fireplaces).

- Never to use heat- or flame-producing items in dangerous proximity to combustible materials.

- To use a wood burner in line with the manufacturer's instructions (landlords must provide these).

- To use only appropriate fuels for the fire or wood burner.

Directory

General

HETAS – UK government-recognised organisation that approves biomass and solid fuel heating appliances, fuels and services
hetas.co.uk

WOODSURE – the UK's only woodfuel certification scheme
woodsure.co.uk

THE GUILD OF MASTER CHIMNEY SWEEPS – chimney sweep services and training
guildofmasterchimneysweeps.co.uk

THE NATIONAL ASSOCIATION OF CHIMNEY SWEEPS
nacs.org.uk

ASSOCIATION OF PROFESSIONAL AND
INDEPENDENT CHIMNEY SWEEPS
apics.org.uk

FORESTRY COMMISSION – information about
scavenging permits, woodland grants and tree
planting, and felling regulations
forestry.gov.uk

DEPARTMENT FOR ENVIRONMENT, FOOD
AND RURAL AFFAIRS – information on
authorized fuels and exempt appliances
smokecontrol.defra.gov.uk

THE FIRE SAFETY ADVICE CENTRE – free fire
safety and fire prevention advice
firesafe.org.uk

WOOD HEAT ASSOCIATION – information on
woodfuel suppliers, and biomass boiler and
stove installers and distributors
woodheatassociation.org.uk

STOVE INDUSTRY ALLIANCE – information
on how to choose a wood-burning stove and
energy efficiency

  stoveindustryalliance.com

BUILDING CONTROL – planning information
on building regulations and how they affect the
installation and use of wood heating

  planningportal.co.uk

Woodburning Stove Manufacturers

Salamander
(specialists in small stoves for small spaces)

  salamanderstoves.com

Charnwood

  charnwood.com

Morso

  morsoe.com/en

Chesneys
  chesneys.co.uk

Flavel
  flavelfires.co.uk

Mendip
  mendipstoves.co.uk

Stovax
  stovax.com

Clearview
  clearviewstoves.com

Saltfire
  woodburningstovesdirect.com

About the Author

Sally Coulthard has been setting fire to things since she was a small, dungareed tomboy. Gently discouraged from a career in professional pyromania, she's now a bestselling author of books about natural history and rural life, including *The Barn*, *A Short History of the World According to Sheep*, *The Hedgehog Handbook* and over twenty more titles. She lives tucked away on a Yorkshire farm where she can burn things without bothering anyone.